...And Now,

THE
GOOD
NEWS

...And Now,

THE GOOD NEWS

20 Years of Inspiring News Stories

GOOD NEWS NETWORK

and Geri Weis-Corbley

Foreword by Ellen K

Good News Network Publishing
Santa Barbara, California

in association with
White Cloud Press
Ashland, Oregon

Good News Network Publishing
PO Box 4303
Santa Barbara, CA 93140
www.goodnewsnetwork.org/publishing

ISBN 978-1-940468-83-9

First Edition 2018

Contents

ANIMALS

INSPIRING

CELEBRITIES

*Thank you to all our fans who have written to us,
shared our stories, volunteered, and joined as members.
You are the heart and soul of our mission.*

*Dedicated with gratitude to Jim Corbley, without
whose support GNN would not have been possible.
Your brilliant editing in the early years taught
me how to be a good writer.*

Foreword

A *Washington Post* article named her "The Good News Guru."

Geri worked in hard news in Washington DC for 10 years and always thought, "There should be more *good* news" in the media. She started the Good News Network over 20 years ago—and we're so glad she did.

When I first left as Ryan Seacrest's co-host to produce and host my own radio morning show at KOST-103.5, and now across the nation, the most common question I'd get was "What is your show going to be about?"

I'd always answer the same way, "I don't know, but it will be all good things."

When my team was hired, it all fell into place. We clicked, and our fondness for each other—and for the listeners—sent positive vibes through the airwaves. Now we have a top rated morning show in Los Angeles, and in 2018 Geri became part of our on-air family.

When I first heard about the Good News Network, I knew I wanted to have Geri on the show. When she came into the studio, we immediately loved her, and now, "The Good News Guru" is an integral part of the show, bringing us her 'good news story of the week'.

As we succeed in adding more 'gas to the good fire' that is already burning in all of us, more great examples of good news will emerge to support our basic message that we can all do really well by doing good!

Geri's Good News Network stories have startled us with kindness and given us hope for humanity. Although it's impossible for us to pick our favorites from among the weekly stories (all of which you can listen to on the Good News Guru's podcast), this new collection of highlights from the past two decades will leave you feeling hopeful, happy, and hooked on Geri!

It's lovely to know there's a Good News Guru in this world.

Ellen K

Preface

Good News Network founder Geri Weis-Corbley

I've always been an optimist. It's in my Swiss–Czech DNA.

When I entered the TV news business in Washington, DC straight out of college, it took about a month for me to notice how the media mostly favored the pessimistic stories. I commented to a colleague, "There should be a 'good news' show." He promptly informed me that "good news doesn't sell."

I didn't believe it. Some of the most successful TV shows and magazines in the 1980s focused on heroes and uplifting stories. The idea never left me that there should be some kind of media outlet where good news could be reliably found.

It resurfaced 15 years later when my son was six years old and I was listening to a particularly gory NPR radio story about the Bosnian War. I looked at him and wondered, "At what point does he start 'hearing' this stuff?"

By that day in 1997 the internet had dawned—and it suddenly dawned on me that I could create a website of good news.

On Labor Day, after teaching myself HTML software, I clicked a 'publish' button and suddenly anyone in the world could read the website I called Good News Network. Instead of CNN (the network I had regularly freelanced for), it would be known as GNN. Instead of "If it bleeds it leads," our motto would be: "If it's good deeds, it leads!"

It was GNN's mission to uplift the world and remind people that there was as much good happening as bad.

Over the next two decades I outlasted some competitors, built a loyal fan base of engaged viewers of all ages, and owned the #1 spot on Google for good or inspiring news. I developed a free app, which earned mostly 5-star reviews, and, thanks to my new co-owning partner whom I adore (the television and film producer Anthony Samadani), our 'Good News Guru' radio segment with Ellen K is now syndicated around the country and available as a podcast. Our newly designed website offers more than good news—it now features Good Talks and Good Gifts, with more to come.

I've always wanted to publish a collection of our best stories in a book. As a tribute to our first 20 years, I hope you will share this edition so that more people will learn about GNN.org as a place online to turn away from the gloom, a legacy brand that proves—once and for all—that good news *does* sell.

And Now, The Good News...

USA

Bank That Lost 66 Workers on 9/11 Has Paid for All Their Kids to Go to College

On Sept. 11, 2001, 66 men and women who worked for the investment banking firm Sandler O'Neill & Partners on the 104th floor in the World Trade Center lost their lives.

In the harrowing days following the terrorist attacks, the company made the decision to set up a foundation to pay college tuition for all the 76 children of their fallen colleagues.

I called the Sandler O'Neill Foundation in 2015 to talk about those children, and learned that 54 young men and women have had their college tuition paid so far, with 22 young men and women still eligible. The 54 who are attending or have attended college have gone to every sort of college imaginable—from Stanford to Notre Dame to community colleges and technical institutes.

The youngest child eligible was born six weeks after September 11. When that child graduates from college, the Sandler O'Neill Foundation will cease to exist, except in memory; but what a resounding memory it will be.

Andy Armstrong was one of the founders of the foundation. Though he did not work for Sandler O'Neill, he was a friend of Sandler's surviving partner, Jimmy Dunne. He and others of Dunne's friends and colleagues – as well as banking competitors – helped set up and endow the foundation.

"We were up and running by the end of the first week," Armstrong says. "We wanted the families of the lost to know that we would always remember, that the passing years would never sweep this under the rug. People donated many millions of dollars to set up the foundation. We have no salaries and no expenses except fees to stay extant."

"I know most of the children who went to college. You wouldn't believe some of the letters they have written in appreciation. I think they particularly appreciate that we remember their mom or dad this way."

I called Jimmy Dunne at Sandler O'Neill to ask him why he instantly did so very much the right thing, the extraordinary thing, when it would have been so easy and normal and understandable to just do enough.

"Because there was a moment in time to stand up," Dunne says, bluntly. "Because we believed that what we did would echo for a hundred years in the families of our people, their kids and their grandkids. Because how we conducted ourselves in those first few hours and days would define who we really were and what we were about."

"Because I knew that if we were not honorable, then we stood for nothing. I concluding immediately that we would not be intimidated, we would not go out of business, we will come back stronger than ever, and be an example of people who worked and lived with honor. And that meant taking care of our people and their children with respect and reverence. So we did that. We figured what we did and how we did it was our way of fighting idiots like bin Laden. You want us to fall apart? Then we will survive and flourish. You want to destroy us? Then we will insist even more on acting with honor. That's what the foundation was for, is for. We want our defiance and reverence to echo for a century, so that the grandchildren of our people will know we stood for something, and acted honorably when it really counted."

Brian Doyle was the editor of Portland Magazine at the University of Portland, and author of 30 books—novels, non-fiction, and essay collections—before he passed away in 2017.

Farmers Stay Silent During Auction So Young Man Can Win Bid on Long-Lost Family Farm

I've had two profoundly humbling days in my life. The first was the day my son was born. The second was that unforgettable day at the Auction House."

This is how David, one of the participants in a session I recently facilitated, answered the question I had just posed to the group: "When in your life have you set a big goal and had no idea at the time how you were going to make it happen?"

Generations before David was born, eighty acres of their small family farm in Nebraska had been separated out and willed to a distant relative. Coming from a long line of farmers David heard this story over and over as a child, and it fueled a passion within him to make the farm whole again.

In 2011, David and his family learned that the precious eighty acres was going to be sold at auction within a couple of weeks. Suddenly at the ripe old age of twenty-something David needed to figure out how to find an extraordinarily large sum of money.

"Even though I dreamt of getting the land back for as long as I could remember, when the day came, I wasn't ready." He knew in his heart he had to give it his very best effort—and after two weeks of meticulous planning, creative thinking and sleepless nights, he and his father came up with their 'best number', and headed for auction.

When they walked through the door of the Auction House that night, their hearts immediately sank. The place was packed with over 200 farmers, most of whom had much larger farms, more resources, and could outbid him and his father many times over. The auctioneer called the session to order and asked for the first bid. David and his dad looked at each other, took a deep breath, and made theirs. The auctioneer acknowledged their bid, and then called for a second.

Silence fell over the room.

After many attempts to solicit another bid, the auctioneer took a break. When they reconvened, a second bid was once again called for; silence. Three times they took breaks, each time they resumed the room remained completely silent. Finally, the auctioneer had no choice but to award David and his father the winning bid. David and his father were stunned—the family farm was once again complete.

The emotion on David's face and in his voice as he told us the story was powerful. The other participants and I leaned forward, hanging on his every word. After David finished his story, I asked him what he thought had occurred in the Auction House that night, and without missing a beat, he looked at me with even more emotion, and said, "Respect."

Like the farmers in the Auction House, the participants and I sat silent for many moments as we contemplated David's answer. "There it is," I thought to myself. "The power of community. Another wonderful example of what's right with our world."

*Lauri Gwilt is co-author and co-host of **The Habit of Celebration**, an e-course from the Celebrate What's Right initiative. (celebratewhatsright.com)*

She Invested 7 Years of Her Life and $60,000 to Free a Stranger from Prison

A 68-year-old New Jersey widow was so convinced of a young man's innocence after reading a news account of his murder conviction that she spent seven years and $60,000 of her own money to see that justice would prevail.

Priscilla Chenoweth had six years of experience as a lawyer, but little experience with criminal trials, before becoming an editor at the New Jersey Law Journal. Yet, she began to investigate the homicide because the convicted boy also had little experience—with gangs, or violence. He had no record, and nice friends. In fact, 150 of his classmates and teachers wrote letters to the judge insisting that the teenager's involvement was impossible.

Chenoweth worked with an unwavering tenacity—reading transcripts, interviewing witnesses, filing motions, and conducting hearings to prove grounds for an appeal.

The mother of three and grandmother of five worked alongside her daughter, Lesley Estevao, who first brought her mom's attention to the case. They enlisted a retired New York City police detective whose pastime is unsolved murders, to contribute his expertise. A second retired police officer helped Estevao—who began calling herself the "kitchen-table investigator"—to locate a key witness who could establish an alibi, a transit officer who remembered seeing the young man just miss a train leaving the station at the time of the murder.

Another lawyer, who also donated his services, worked with Mrs. Chenoweth at the retrial in 1998, and together they won an acquittal.

Mrs. Chenoweth stuck by the brave young man's side through the seven-year ordeal, offering as much support as she could. Throughout and since, he has never failed to send her a Mother's Day card.

The young man was subsequently compensated by the State of New York for his wrongful imprisonment. He finished his education and became an engineer. Chenoweth's daughter Lesley is now an attorney herself, and is continuing her mom's crusade as founding director of the Last Resort Exoneration Project at Seton Hall University's law school.

Instead of Another Protest, 'Black Lives Matter' Joined Police For a Barbecue

Photo courtesy of Javier Guete

In the summer of 2016, when urban areas across America erupted with racial tension, one city in Kansas was proud of their Black Lives Matter protest, during which no one was hurt or arrested, and no property was damaged. Protestors praised the Wichita police force for their efforts in allowing voices and first amendment rights to be expressed—and things only got better from there.

Plans for a second BLM protest the next Sunday were changed to a community cookout, after leaders met with Police Chief Gordon Ramsay the day after the demonstration. Ramsay said he and the mayor would raise the money to organize a barbecue for the city's law enforcement professionals and the community at large.

Both sides agreed it was a great first step toward healing and building a bond between those in blue and those who want to end injustice.

Any and all were invited to attend the cookout at McAdams Park—billed as the 'First Steps Barbecue.'

Among hamburgers and hot dogs, basketball and dancing, a bond was forged with fun; during a question-and-answer session about racial profiling and transparency, that bond was further strengthened with communication.

Ramsay vowed that despite personnel shortages in the department, he would continue to make sure officers are properly trained in cultural competency, while he tries to free up more time for officers to engage in this type of community involvement.

Captain's Crew is Saved By Ten-Dollar Bill—and an American Miracle

Captain Eddie Max Stoval III (inset left) engineered the delivery of 12,000 lbs of supplies, 104,000 gallons of water, and 23,000 gallons of diesel to Captain Ahmed (right) and his crew stranded on the Delta Pride.

By the time 22 Pakistani sailors had made it to safe harbor off the tip of Texas on the eve of Thanksgiving in 1998, they had no fuel, no power, no water, no passports, and were starving. They had been surviving on one hope—instilled in them by their young captain—to make it to U.S. waters.

Dying without any water, anchored at open sea with no one to help them, the Muslim captain found a ten dollar bill in his drawer. "I don't know how it got there. I had no money for many months."

Instantly the words, 'In God We Trust' caught his eyes. "I never paid any attention to these words but this time they were so attracting to me," he told GNN. "I felt in my heart that this was the answer to my prayers, like advice from God: go to the United States and people can help you out there."

Using buckets, the crew amassed the dregs of 'empty' fuel tanks—hundreds of gallons that lie below the suction line—and fired a torch to heat the heavy fuel to get the engines started one more time.

Several days into the journey, and on Thanksgiving Eve, Captain Eddie Max Stovall, III, from Port Isabel, Texas, heard their pleas for help. He called them back on his radio and 36-year-old Captain Maqsood Ahmed told the dire tale of how their passports and ship's papers had been taken as collateral for unpaid harbor fees in Mexico after the Pakistani shipping company that owned the 740-foot cargo ship claimed bankruptcy. The crew, effectively left stranded, was owed up to two years of back wages.

Eddie Stovall says, "I'm no 'do-gooder', but I know what it's like to be without food or water at sea. I couldn't NOT do something."

Within a few hours that Sunday he had turned their tragedy into a rescue story for the ages.

He spent $500 of his own money on food and water, which he delivered to them in his boat. The 39-year-old seaman said they were so weak from hunger, "They couldn't even lift up the heaving line with a 5-gallon jug of water attached—we had to break it down into gallons."

He called his fellow captains at the Propeller Club of the U.S., and the International Seamen's Club to start collecting funds and fuel for the generator, and he formed a coalition of locals and churches, who donated frozen food and many other supplies.

As Stovall's heart went out to them, his bride's did too. Just married that same week, she felt strongly that the homesick sailors, who had been away from Pakistan for 18-27 months, should get a chance to talk to their families again. So the newlyweds hired a marine VHF radio operator to patch 22 calls home.

Capt. Ahmed recalls, "Families were crying, children were crying because they didn't know if we were alive or dead."

30 minutes later, the marine operator called the Stovalls back after his boss learned what was going on and said there would be no charge for the overseas calls.

"A lot of people gave," Stovall told us when we talked to him again 20 years later. In a 3-inch-thick scrapbook he kept a ledger of everyone who donated, and pasted all the press clippings about the rescue effort (and the nine months of legal proceedings that followed). "You know, the people who had the least, gave the most."

A reverend from the Seamen's Church of New York City even raised the money to finally fly them back home.

The ordeal has sealed Ahmed's love for Americans. "The people are so loving and so caring. They are more open-hearted here than in other countries."

"You know, people don't believe in miracles. But I believe," he exclaimed. "I believe now."

Veteran Homelessness Was Ended in Virginia, The First State to Do It

Virginia became the first state in the U.S. to be certified as effectively ending homelessness among military veterans. Announced on Veteran's Day 2015, Virginia adopted the principles of 'Housing First'—providing shelter before addressing the underlying cause of the homelessness. They offered the housing, in addition to support services to maintain stability, and were able to lift 1,432 vets off the streets in a single year.

WORLD

Man Single-handedly Carves a Road Through a Mountain to Help His Village

Photo courtesy of Milaap.org

For years, he was called a madman for toiling away on the rocks. But Dashrath Manjhi was not crazy. His quest to break a path through a small mountain to benefit his entire village is now legendary because he carved an entire road with hand tools—and it took him 22 years.

Manjhi began his extraordinary task in 1960, after his wife was injured while trekking up the side of the rocky incline. He then had to hike around the mountains over 40 miles to reach the nearest hospital, by which time his wife had died.

The widowed laborer from Gehlour Hills, in Bihar, India, ached for his people to have easier access to doctors, schools, and opportunity. Armed with only a sledge hammer, a chisel, and a crowbar, he single-handedly began hacking through the 300-foot mountain that isolated his village from the nearest town.

"People told Manjhi that he wouldn't be able to do it," said Dahu Manjhi, the man's nephew, "that he is a poor man who just needs to earn and eat."

He sold the family's three goats to buy the tools and worked every day on the project to make it successful. After plowing fields for others in the morning, he would work on his road all evening and throughout the night.

He toiled from 1960 to 1982, having developed his own technique. He burned firewood on the rocks, then sprinkled water on the heated surface, which cracked the boulders, making it possible to reduce them to rubble.

Finally, the road was completed. With sides 25 feet high, the road is 30 feet wide and 360 feet in length. Because of his singular dedication, the distance to public services was reduced from 40 miles (70km) to just one.

It has been 36 years since the "Mountain Man," as he was called, completed the road. The feat brought the Gehlour man international acclaim. After he died of cancer in 2007, Bihar's Chief Minister gave him a State funeral. Though many believe he deserved it, he never received the Bharat Ratna, the nation's highest civilian honor that recognizes "exceptional service" in the community.

"Now the whole society is worshiping him," said Dahu, "but only after he died."

Though his region now has easier access to hospitals and the outside world, people of his village still live in poverty. Carrying on the Mountain Man's broader vision for economic progress, Manjhi's life-long friend committed to opening a trade school in the village, setting up the Dashrath Manjhi Welfare Trust to inspire young people and offer meaningful education to better their lives.

Milaap.org, a crowdfunding platform, successfully raised the funds that the 82-year-old social worker Ram Charit Prasad needed.

"I did what I could through my limited means," said Ram Charit, "but only with the support of people like you could we take it forward, and break through the mountain."

This Village in India Plants 111 Trees Whenever a Girl is Born

Typically in Asian cultures, the birth of a girl is considered an unfortunate responsibility because of the dowry system that puts financial stress on the parents' future. For this reason, daughters were never as celebrated as sons.

But in one village in India, the residents celebrate with a unique ritual of planting one hundred and eleven fruit trees.

Through this tradition, every time a girl is born, the people of Piplantri, Rajasthan, buck the historical prejudice against daughters and beautify their homeland at the same time.

The village's former leader Shyam Sundar Palaiwal first started the practice in 2006 to honor his deceased daughter Kiran. Wanting to ensure the future protection and care of female children in the village, he launched a tradition that would not only enhance the local environment but also raise money for the girls' families. The noble custom has endured for over a decade.

In order to make sure that the young ladies are always provided for, the villagers come together to raise 30,000 rupees ($450) to set aside as each girl's fund for the next twenty years. The children's parents then reciprocate the gesture by signing an oath that their daughter will not be married until she has reached the age of 18 and received an education.

These incredible actions serve as more than just hope for the future of gender equality in India. Planting the fruit trees has ensured that resources will be available for the growing population of the village.

From one man's compassion, more than a quarter of a million trees have been planted.

Thousands of Muslims Form 'Human Shield' Protecting Christians, Who Return the Favor

Following a devastating terrorist bombing in Egypt at a Christian church during their holy holiday in January 2011, thousands of Muslims, including the two sons of then-President Hosni Mubarak, arrived a week later to act as "human shields" protecting those attending mass from a possible second attack. Thousands held hands to form a ring around the church.

Days later, to repay the kindness, Christians formed a circle around the Muslim men who were praying outside, to defend them against retaliation.

'Water Gandhi' of India Turns Dust Bowls Into Lush Villages Using Ancient Ways

Through a stroke of fate, a man now called 'The Water Gandhi of India' began turning abandoned, impoverished 'dust bowls' into lush villages bustling with life again, using an ancient method of rainwater harvesting.

30 years ago, Rajendra Singh went to the poverty-stricken state of Rajasthan with the aim of setting up health clinics. He was told by villagers, however, that their greatest need was not health care, but water. Their wells had dried up. Soon afterward, crops wilted, rivers and forests disappeared, and many able-bodied villagers left in search of work in the cities. Women, children and the elderly were left behind without hope, as their villages became barren dust bowls.

So, instead of clinics, Singh showed them how to build johads, traditional earthen dams—and the results proved wildly successful.

In the two decades since he arrived, 8,600 johads have been built to collect water for 1,000 villages across the state. Nature then took over, replenishing the groundwater. Rivers began flowing again and the forest coverage increased, bringing back animals like the antelope, and even the majestic peacock, once on the verge of extinction here. Women, formerly burdened with carrying water from miles away, now had time for other things.

Residents came to revere him, and in 2015 Singh was honored with the $150,000 Stockholm Water Prize for his work.

Thanks to the 'Water man of India' and his non-profit Tarun Bharat Sangh, many of the country's poorest communities are now prosperous—empowered once again by agricultural livelihoods and more free time for chasing rainbows.

Norway Muslims Form Human Shield Around Jewish Synagogue

European Jews faced rising anti-Semitism in some countries, but multiculturalism is also on the rise. In February 2015, more than 1,000 Muslims and their supporters formed a human shield around Oslo's synagogue, offering protection and solidarity with Jews following a violent attack in Copenhagen.

Chanting "No to anti-Semitism. No to Islamophobia," the defenders formed what they called a ring of peace during the event organized on Facebook.

"Humanity is one, and we are here to demonstrate that," Zeeshan Abdullah, one of the organizers, told the crowd of Muslim immigrants and ethnic Norwegians who filled the streets around Oslo's only synagogue.

An English translation of the Facebook page reads: "Islam is about protecting our brothers and sisters, regardless of which religion they belong to. Islam is about rising above hate and never sinking to the same level as the haters . . . Muslims want to show that we deeply deplore all types of hatred of Jews, and that we are there to support them."

Mom Forgives the Unforgivable, Works With Daughter's Killers to Bring Hope to Desperate Community

Photo © Johanna Baldwin

One of the most remarkable stories of forgiveness had its sad beginning 25 years ago, on Aug 26, 1993. We reached out to the California woman whose inspiring daughter gave her life to create positive change for a beautiful yet struggling country, leading her parents to follow in her footsteps.

Amy Biehl was a bright, determined Stanford graduate who ventured to South Africa on a Fulbright scholarship to work in the anti-apartheid movement during its explosive final months before Mandela became president.

She worked alongside her black comrades to register voters, and she longed to address the poverty of their squalid townships, believing that economic change was critical for any meaningful transformation. She had been driving two co-workers home when the blue-eyed blonde became a target for four angry youths who'd just left a rally where militants were calling for the death of privileged white settlers.

Despite the desperate objections of her ANC colleagues that she was "a comrade," Amy was stabbed to death on a road in Guguletu township on the very corner that her parents would soon be calling "The Spot of Hope."

Peter and Linda Biehl left their gated community in wealthy Orange County, motivated and haunted by Amy's diaries. They flew to Cape Town and toured the townships where Amy worked and talked with her friends about the unemployment problem. Peter was a businessman, and with money pouring in to honor their daughter's noble cause, they began to organize one development project after another—welding, sewing, a print shop, a bakery, a construction company, sports facilities, and adult literacy programs.

But the most startling development of all was the relationship that developed between Amy's parents and her killers.

"People say, 'well I couldn't get together with people that harmed my loved one,' but forgiveness is really about liberating yourself—letting go, so you can be free of hate and bitterness. It's really a one-way street that doesn't need the other person to do anything."

The Biehls were raised with a Christian faith that valued forgiveness and it was important to them that they not be hypocritical: "Often people aren't able to live up to their Christian values—or their Muslim values or Jewish values. It was important that we don't say one thing and do something else."

The Biehls knew that amnesty would be granted to the young men whose crimes were politically motivated, as part of the healing process of that country's Nobel Peace Prize-winning Truth and Reconciliation Commission.

"We did not expect to have a relationship with them, but two of the young men, after they were released from prison, saw that things hadn't changed in their community, and they wanted to help. They had the courage to come to us, to our Foundation, which was bringing jobs to young people—and we admired that," Linda Biehl told Good News Network by telephone from Cape Town.

Easy Nofomela and Ntobeko Peni began working for the Amy Biehl Foundation. Easy still works there today.

"As time went on we became very close," she continued. "I'm very proud of Easy and Ntobeko. They traveled to America with me to speak at conferences and it's been very positive."

"They call me 'Makulu,'" Linda laughed, explaining it means grandmother. "They kind of adopted us into their village—it was pretty amazing. That is Amy's gift to all of us—she brought us all together."

Ntobeko doesn't know how Amy's parents found it in their hearts to forgive him, but he told one reporter that it has greatly enriched his life. "I will never forget the kindness they have shown me when they had every reason to hate me."

Read more about the unlikely friendship at GNN.org. You can donate to the Foundation at www.amybiehl.org or follow USAABF on Facebook.

ANIMALS

Pup Deemed 'Too Friendly' for Police Work Finds Appropriate New Job

This German shepherd wasn't cut out for the life of a police dog—but he's found a much more suitable line of work, thanks to the government of Queensland, Australia.

Gavel was sacked after undergoing a police dog training course because he was more keen on socializing with perpetrators than being "professional."

There's no need to worry about Gavel's future, however, because he's now employed as Queensland's first ever official Vice-Regal dog for the Government House.

Since he started working for Governor Paul de Jersey in February 2017, the pup has become the most popular political figure in town.

When he's not attending important meetings as an official representative of the office or cheering for Queensland sports teams, he's snuggling with the staff, greeting visitors, and spreading cheer wherever he goes—a much more fitting role for him than ferociously fighting on the frontlines.

Dog Chained Up During Flood Gets Adopted by the Man Who Saved Her

The only thing now flooding around this poor Texan pup is tender loving care.

Sheriff Troy Nehls and a news crew from KPRC in Fort Bend County discovered the dog while surveying heavy flooding in 2016. The dog was so overcome by the rising waters that only her head could be seen poking out above the surface.

When Nehls and the journalists approached the distressed animal, they realized that the dog was unable to swim away because she was tied to a porch.

Nehls and one of the journalists then plunged into the water, untied the dog's leash, and hauled the waterlogged pup into the rescue boat.

After taking her to the Humane Society where she was evaluated and deemed healthy, journalists reached out to the former owner of the dog who had skipped town to flee the hurricane. The man said that he did not believe the floodwaters would be high enough to harm the hound. He was allegedly unable to return to the house because of the flooding, but he was more than happy to relinquish ownership of the dog.

Sheriff Nehls's family then agreed to adopt the dog and give her a loving home.

Additionally, they decided to name the dog Archer after the journalist who helped save her.

"There's a bond this dog and I have that will remain with us," Nehls told a reporter. "She's not tied up to a front porch. She's in a home that is comfortable, she's sleeping on a bed, and she gets constant attention from the family."

Archer can now rest happily on higher ground for the rest of her days.

Man Builds Tiny 'Life Jacket' To Save Beloved Pet Goldfish

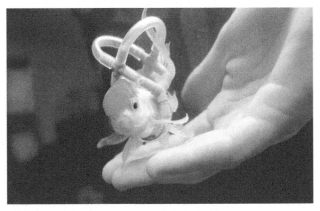

SWNS

A goldfish named Einstein wasn't able to do his tricks anymore, like swimming through hoops—a feat orchestrated by Leighton Naylor using a wand.

Little Einstein was diagnosed with a bladder infection, which severely inhibited his ability to move.

Rather than just giving him the big flush, Leighton, from Blackpool, England, made him an underwater 'life jacket' from recycled tubing that proved to work just swimmingly.

His care for the tiny creature likely inspired others to show similar affection, after his YouTube video and news reports were viewed worldwide.

Stork Flies 5,000 Miles Every Year To Be With Injured Soul Mate

If you don't believe in long-lasting love, then you've never heard about the famous Romeo and Juliet of birds.

Ever since Malena the stork had her wing shot by a hunter in 1993, she has been unable to join her soul mate on his 5,000 mile migration from Eastern Europe to South Africa.

But that doesn't stop her partner, Klepetan, from coming back every year like clockwork to be alongside his injured love in Slavonski Brod, Croatia.

The celebrity couple has raised more than 40 chicks in the 14 years they've been together—and they're so beloved by village residents, that there's a live internet feed of their reunion running every spring.

A village school teacher found Malena lying on her side in the road almost two decades ago, and he has always cared for her in Klepetan's absence. Every winter, the warm-weather Malena is allowed to stay in the house with his family, while during the summer, she resides in a nest that he's built on his roof.

Storks aren't famous for their long-term mating practices, but they have been known to stay mostly monogamous if they find the right companion.

Other males have tried to woo Malena in Klepetan's absence, but she has always chased off the presumptuous birds so she can continue waiting for her one true love.

Baby Tortoises Survive on Galapagos Island for First Time in 100 Years

During a December 2015 survey of giant tortoises on a Galapagos island, conservationists discovered the first hatchlings to have survived in the wild in over a century.

The Pinzón Island saddleback giant tortoise was on the brink of extinction by the 1960s when there were only around 100 animals left in existence. The only thing saving the species was the longevity of the adults, which enjoy lifespans of more than 100 years.

The exciting find of ten baby tortoises was the direct result of a rat eradication campaign completed two years earlier on Pinzón, when helicopters criss-crossed the island dropping rat bait, which was non-toxic to the native flora and fauna.

Black rats that were accidentally introduced to the Equadorian island chain by pirates and whalers in the 17th and 18th centuries had decimated the tortoise population. In fact, zero hatchlings could survive during a period of almost 150 years, but the Charles Darwin Foundation and Galapagos National Park had carefully gathered some eggs to hatch and rear in captivity.

Today, thanks to the rat eradication program, the adult saddleback tortoises (Chelonoidis ephippium) have begun to repopulate the island unaided, like they did centuries ago.

Flight Attendant Adopts Stray Dog That Always Awaited Her Return From Countries Abroad

When Olivia Sievers paid attention to this poor homeless pooch outside her hotel, it was love at first sight—afterwards, he only had puppy eyes for her.

In February 2016, the German flight attendant flew to Argentina for business. On her way to the Hilton in Buenos Aires, she met the amiable stray for the first time and offered him some love and attention. The dog refused to leave her side and followed her all the way to the hotel, hanging out with her for two days whenever she left the building.

When it was time for Olivia to fly back to Germany, she sadly bid a fond farewell to her new friend expecting to never see him again.

But in April she returned and they reunited for two more days. They spent many hours walking miles together—and he always followed her back to the hotel.

Afterward, she didn't fly back to Buenos Aires for three months. When she returned in July, she wanted to sleep for a few hours and planned to search for the dog and continue trying to find him a home.

When she came down to the lobby, he was already sitting in front of the Hilton's glass doors.

'How did he know I was back,' she wondered.

"The Hotel staff told me later that day, that he was sitting in front of the hotel for three months—sometimes returning a few times a day—looking for me."

This time, she tried to arrange an adoption with a manager in a nearby hotel in San Telmo. She delivered the dog, whom he named Rubio, but after one week he escaped, faithfully backtracking the 1.7 kilometers to join the flight attendant once more at the hotel in Puerto Madero.

Olivia realized their long-distance relationship had to end.

To save Rubio from his dangerous life as a street dog, she decided to adopt the hound herself, bringing him all the way home to Germany. He has settled in happily with her other pooches and now spends long afternoons romping in the backyard never worrying about where in the world Olivia might be.

*An audio book about their extraordinary friendship, **Love without Borders: Rubio, the most loyal dog of the world** is available on Amazon.*

INSPIRING

Grieving Man Can Finally Sleep Again, After Girl Reaches Out in Grocery Store

See more photos on Facebook.com/NorahandMr.Dan

Kids are taught in schools not to talk to strangers—but little Norah Wood did the exact opposite and was able to heal a grieving, lonely man.

Norah and her mom, Tara, were in the grocery store shopping for cupcakes to celebrate Norah's fourth birthday when the little girl spotted an old man plodding through the aisles.

"Her face lit up like the sun, she waved excitedly, and said 'Hi old person! It's my birfday today!'" Tara wrote on Facebook.

Guarded at first, he soon softened under her spell.

According to her mother, the outgoing child is a self-proclaimed senior lover: "I like old peoples the best 'cos they walk slow like I walk slow and they has soft skin . . . They all gonna die soon so I'm gonna love 'em all up before they is died."

The 4-year-old then asked if they could take a picture together for her birthday. Though initially surprised by the request, he happily obliged.

"We thanked 'Mr. Dan' for taking time to spend a few minutes of his day with us. He teared up and said 'No, thank YOU. This has been the best day I've had in a long time. You've made me so happy, Ms. Norah.'"

Tara posted the photos to Facebook where they were shared thousands of times. Eventually, one user wrote saying that Dan's wife had passed away a few months ago and he was probably appreciative of the company.

Touched by the story, Tara reached out to the widower and asked if she and Norah could come by for a visit.

The 4-year-old and the senior ended up spending three hours over a table of crayons and paper.

Dan later admitted that he hadn't been able to sleep properly since his wife died—but after meeting Norah, he was slumbering uninterrupted every night. He believes that though she may not know it, the little girl healed him with her love.

Since their first play date in the spring of 2016, Dan Peterson has become part of the Wood family and Norah visits him weekly at his Georgia home.

The 83-year-old realized just how much the youngster cared for him after she recently knocked on his door. When he opened it, she started hugging him—and wouldn't let go.

The little girl was distraught because it took him so long to open the door, and she was wondering if something had happened to him.

In her short life, she can't remember being without him—and, since that fateful day in the grocery store, the old man can't remember a time when he's slept so well.

Pilot Refuses to Depart Until Delayed Man Bound for His Grandson's Funeral Can Board

A man stuck in airport security gridlock was finally able to say farewell to his murdered grandson after a Southwest Airline pilot refused to depart from the gate without him.

The man, whose 3-year-old grandson was to have life-support turned off that night, thought he arrived early enough—two hours ahead of departure for a domestic flight.

But despite explaining his predicament to the security staff, he said that no one cared at all to help him through the long lines to ensure he could board before takeoff.

Fortunately, his wife had purchased the flight from a caring airline, and she had told the ticketing agent about the tragic reason for his trip.

Upon arrival at his gate, 12 minutes late, shoes in hand and out of breath, he was greeted by Southwest Air personnel: "Are you Mark? We held the plane for you and we're so sorry about the loss of your grandson."

As the pilot walked him down the jetway to the plane, the grieving grandfather thanked him for the kindness.

The pilot summed up his decision, saying, "They can't go anywhere without me, and I wasn't going anywhere without you."

Courtesy of Elliott Advocacy / elliott.org

Subway Passengers Join Together to Prepare Anxious Man For Job Interview

Canadians really are just as kind as they're fabled to be.

When Salma Hamidi was leaving Finch subway station in North York, Ontario, an anxious Latino man entered the car, put his head in his hands, and nervously started saying "Oh God."

"The Russian guy sitting beside him asked if everything was ok, in a pretty heavy accent," Salma wrote on Facebook.

He answered that he had a horrible headache and was running late for an interview.

Salma offered him an Advil out of her purse, which he accepted with a word of thanks, but since he had nothing to wash it down with, he said he would take it later.

"The Middle Eastern woman sitting beside me wearing [a] hijab, took out a juice box from her kid's backpack and gave it to him telling him that if he takes it now he'll feel better by the time he gets to the interview."

The Russian man started advising him to walk confidently and tie his hair back if he could. A Chinese teenager sitting nearby overheard his remark and handed the Latino a hair tie from off her wrist.

"I told him if he gets in late, to apologize but not bring excuses. Nobody likes excuses."

"The Muslim lady told him to smile a lot, people trust easier when you smile."

When the man's stop finally arrived, he exited the car and his fellow passengers waved and wished him good luck as they all basked in the air of kindness.

Salma summed up her national pride with a wink: "Now if THIS isn't the ultimate Canadian experience short of a beaver walking into a bar holding a jar of maple syrup, I don't know what is!"

Women Encircle a Crying Mom Whose Toddler Was Having a Meltdown at the Airport

While airports might typically act as a spark plug for stress, they can also be places where strangers assist during the worst moments of travel anxiety.

One such incident happened to Beth Bornstein Dunnington when she was flying out of Los Angeles earlier this month.

The mom from Waimea, Hawaii was at LAX waiting to board her flight to Portland. As she was in the departure area alongside a crowd of other travelers waiting for their own flights, she saw a mother who was having some problems with her son.

Dunnington wrote on Facebook: "A toddler who looked to be eighteen or so months old was having a total meltdown, running between the seats, kicking and screaming, then lying on the ground, refusing to board the plane."

"His young mom, who was clearly pregnant and traveling alone with her son, became completely overwhelmed . . . she couldn't pick him up because he was so upset, he kept running away from her, then lying down on the ground, kicking and screaming again."

"The mother finally sat down on the floor and put her head in her hands, with her kid next to her still having a meltdown, and started crying."

Dunnington was then heartened by what happened next.

Six or seven women from around the boarding area convened on the young mother, forming a little circle around her and her toddler, and each woman did something to help calm down the distressed duo.

"I sang 'The Itsy Bitsy Spider' to the little boy... one woman had an orange that she peeled; one woman had a little toy in her bag that she let the toddler play with; another woman gave the mom a bottle of water. Someone else helped the mom get the kid's sippy cup out of her bag and give it to him."

Though the women did not exchange words over their common goal, they were able to calm down the mother and her toddler until they were successfully able to get on the plane.

"After they went through the door we all went back to our separate seats and didn't talk about it; we were strangers, gathering to solve something."

"It occurred to me that a circle of women, with a mission, can save the world. I will never forget that moment," she added.

Cop Goes Undercover in Wheelchair to Look for Bad News, Finds Only Good News Instead

As part of an undercover operation, a Vancouver police sergeant in British Columbia grew some facial hair and borrowed an expensive wheelchair, making him an "easy mark" for criminals to snatch the bag on his lap.

Over the course of five days, instead of strangers snatching money from his open fanny pack, around 300 people made contact to ask if he had someone to care for him, to find out if he needed food, or to offer money.

At one point, a man crouched over him and reached for the fanny pack, making the officer nervous—but all he did was zip it shut and offer instructions to be more careful.

CELEBRITIES

Rick Steves Sacrifices Nest Egg to House Dozens of Homeless Women and Children

YWCA Director Mary Anne Dillon and Rick Steves
© Natalie Covate, My Edmonds News

Travel guide guru Rick Steves has given a $4 million apartment complex to homeless women and children who need housing.

Steves realized early on the importance of affordable housing while traveling through Europe as an adventurous young man.

He described his personal backpacking trip as "Europe Through the Gutter," a wandering teen embarking on the daily challenge of finding cheap (in other words, free) places to sleep.

With his rail pass, he'd sleep on trains, ferries, the pews of Greek churches, the concrete floors of Dutch construction projects, and in barns at the edge of unaffordable Swiss alpine resorts.

"How else would a white, middle-class American kid gain a firsthand appreciation for the value of a safe and comfortable place to sleep?"

Twenty years ago, he devised an altruistic scheme whereby he could put his retirement savings not into a bank to accrue interest, but into cheap apartments that could house struggling neighbors in Lynnwood, Washington. The money would be assisting others while, at the same time, earning more for his own future, whenever property values rose.

"Rather than collecting rent, my 'income' would be the joy of housing otherwise desperate people," Steves explained on his travel blog. "I found this a creative, compassionate and more enlightened way to 'invest' while retaining my long-term security."

Thus, the 24-unit Trinity Place apartments began housing single moms who were recovering from drug addiction and ready to get custody of their children back.

"Imagine the joy of knowing that I could provide a simple two-bedroom apartment for a mom and her kids as she fought to get her life back on track."

But in 2017, Steves's generosity rose to a whole new level. He took his affordable housing project one step further and donated the entire apartment complex to the YWCA. The nonprofit group, which ran the facility since 2005, will now be able to plan for the future, knowing that the facility is theirs to keep.

Since then, Steves has made several more donations to local projects: a $1 million pledge to the Edmonds Center for the Arts; $2 million for a new Edmonds senior and community center; and $2 million for a community center at Trinity Lutheran Church in Lynnwood. He also donates nationally to drug policy reform and Bread for the World—but no project moved his heart quite like the one that now provides a safe, warm roof over the heads of moms and their kids.

Follow Rick's latest news at blog.ricksteves.com

Dolly Parton Quietly Gives Away 100 Millionth Book to Children

The U.S. Library of Congress in Washington D.C. honored country singer and actress Dolly Parton this year to mark a little known milestone in her life—the 100 millionth book she quietly donated to children.

The 'Nation's Library' highlighted her nonprofit group, Imagination Library, founded more than two decades ago with the goal of giving books to kids around the world.

"Of all the things I've done in my life—and it's been a lot 'cause I've been around a long time—this is one of the most precious things and the proudest I am of any program," Dolly told the gathered audience of wee ones and adults.

She engaged the audience during the celebration by reading—and singing—her children's book, derived from an original song, "A Coat of Many Colors," about a child who loved wearing the coat her momma quilted from rags.

Known as 'The Book Lady' by the children who receive her gifts, she started the program to honor her father. He couldn't read, yet he was the "smartest man" she ever knew.

19-Year-old French Superstar Donates Every Penny of $500,000 Earned in World Cup

The French soccer team claimed a 4-2 victory over Croatia in the 2018 World Cup final, but one of their wonderkids is winning hearts for showing his true character off the field.

19-year-old forward Kylian Mbappe earned roughly $22,500 for each of the seven games that France played in the World Cup. On top of that, he was given a $350,000 bonus when his team won the tournament, bringing the total to more than a half million dollars.

But instead of spending his winnings on a Bugatti Roadster, the athlete known as the best young player in the world is donating every Euro to a charity—Premiers de Cordee—which helps disabled and hospitalized children to enjoy sports.

Mbappe not only donates his money to the charity, he spends time with the youth, always finding the right words to encourage them. It seems the teen, whose talent is being compared to Pelé, enjoys the encounters even more than the star-struck kids themselves.

Robert Downey Jr. Shows His True Heart to a Bleeding Stranger

I'm willing to go out on a limb here and guess that most stories of kindness do not begin with celebrity bad boys. Mine does.

His name is Robert Downey Jr.

You've probably heard of him. You may or may not be a fan, but I am, and I was a fan in the early 90's when this story takes place.

It was at a garden party for the ACLU of Southern California. My stepmother was the executive director, which is why I was in attendance without having to pay the $150 fee. It's not that I don't support the ACLU, it's that I was barely twenty and had no money to speak of.

I was escorting my grandmother. There isn't enough room in this essay to explain to you everything she was, I would need volumes, so for the sake of brevity I will tell you that she was beautiful even in her eighties, vain as the day is long, and whip smart, though her particular sort of intelligence did not encompass recognizing young celebrities.

I pointed out Robert Downey Jr. to her when he arrived, in a gorgeous cream-colored linen suit, with

Sarah Jessica Parker on his arm. My grandmother shrugged, far more interested in piling her paper plate with various unidentifiable cheeses cut into cubes. He wasn't Cary Grant or Gregory Peck. What did she care?

The afternoon's main honoree was Ron Kovic, whose story of his time in the Vietnam War, which had left him confined to a wheelchair, had recently been immortalized in the Oliver Stone film *Born on the Fourth of July*. I mention his mobility because it played an unwitting role in what happened next.

We made our way to our folding chairs in the garden with our paper plates and cubed cheeses and we watched my stepmother give one of her eloquent speeches and a plea for donations. Then, Ron Kovic took the podium, and he was mesmerizing, and when it was all over we stood up to leave, and my grandmother tripped.

We'd been sitting in the front row (nepotism has its privileges) and when she tripped she fell smack into the ramp that provided Ron Kovic with access to the stage. I didn't know that wheelchair ramps have sharp edges, but they do, and it sliced her shin right open.

The volume of blood was staggering.

I'd like to be able to tell you that I raced into action; that I quickly took control of the situation, tending to my grandmother and calling for the ambulance that was so obviously needed, but I didn't.

I sat down and put my head between my knees because I thought I was going to faint. Did I mention the blood?

Luckily, somebody did take control of the situation, and that person was Robert Downey Jr.

He ordered someone to call an ambulance. Another to bring a glass of water. Another to fetch a blanket. He took off his gorgeous linen jacket and he rolled up his sleeves and he grabbed hold of my grandmother's leg, and then he took that jacket that I'd assumed he'd taken off only to it keep out of the way, and he tied it around her wound. I watched the cream colored linen turn scarlet with her blood.

He told her not to worry. He told her it would be alright. He knew, instinctively, how to speak to her, how to distract her, how to play to her vanity. He held onto her calf and he whistled. He told her how stunning her legs were.

She said to him, to my humiliation: "My granddaughter tells me you're a famous actor but I've never heard of you."

He stayed with her until the ambulance came and then he walked alongside the stretcher holding her hand and telling her she was breaking his heart by leaving the party so early, just as they were getting to know each other. He waved to her as they closed the doors. "Don't forget to call me, Silvia," he said. "We'll do lunch."

He was a movie star, after all.

Believe it or not, I hurried into the ambulance without saying a word. I was too embarrassed and too shy to thank him.

We all have things we wish we'd said. Moments we'd like to return to and do differently. Rarely do we get the chance to make up for those times that words failed us. But I did. Many years later.

I should mention here that when Robert Downey Jr. was in prison for being a drug addict (which strikes me as absurd and cruel, but that's the topic for a different essay), I thought of writing to him. Of reminding him of that day when he was humanity personified. When he was the best of what we each can be. When he was the kindest of strangers.

But I didn't. Some fifteen years after that garden party, ten years after my grandmother had died and five since he'd been released from prison, I saw him in a restaurant.

I grew up in Los Angeles where celebrity sightings are commonplace and where I was raised to respect people's privacy and never bother someone while they're out having a meal, but on this day I decided to abandon the code of the native Angeleno, and my own shyness, and I approached his table.

I said to him, "I don't have any idea if you remember this . . ." and I told him the story.

He remembered.

"I just wanted to thank you," I said. "And I wanted to tell you that it was simply the kindest act I've ever witnessed."

He stood up and he took both of my hands in his and he looked into my eyes and he said, "You have absolutely no idea how much I needed to hear that today."

*Dana Reinhardt is the author of **A Brief Chapter in My Impossible Life**, **Harmless**, **How to Build a House**, **The Things a Brother Knows**, and **We Are the Goldens**. (www.danareinhardt.net)*

Famous Author Invites 300 Random Strangers to His Home for Thanksgiving Dinner

Victor Villaseñor believes all people in this world are one big family.

In November 1992, he proved it by inviting any and all strangers who wanted to come for a Thanksgiving meal to his Oceanside, California mansion.

The Pulitzer Prize-nominated author of *Rain of Gold*—a 'Latino Roots' account of his family history—placed fliers announcing the event at local bookstores. And by word of mouth the news spread until hundreds of strangers landed on his doorstep that Sunday afternoon.

Why go to all the trouble? Because Victor wants to promote harmony; he believes that peace on Earth begins with a hug. And there was plenty of hugging at his Thanksgiving celebration.

Each and every arrival to his exquisitely decorated 19-room home is greeted by Villaseñor with a hug and kiss. They come bearing trays of roasted turkey, tamales, and desserts. They lounge on his sofas and traipse down the halls and stand in line to use his private bathroom. He even personally guides a group across the grounds to his mother's home to use her bathroom when the queue in front of his own grows too long.

After dinner the author/lecturer gathers the guests on his front lawn to share a passionate speech about the good deeds which abound in life but never make the headlines:

"The last 5,000 years have been mostly peace and harmony—not war and violence. History creates a lie, an illusion. In reality, history is only 10 percent violence. Ninety percent has been good: cooking and birth and family and kids."

The smiles turn to laughter when he challenges them each to hug the stranger standing next to them, to look directly in their eyes. As the crowd begins to buzz with light-heartedness, he shouts, "Not only is peace and harmony possible, it's impossible to stop it!"

The cheers erupt.

"We've got to trust in the good that's inside us."

Days later, when questioned by reporters about whether anything had been stolen from his home, he answered, "We haven't looked. I'm just working on the assumption that no one would take anything. In fact, we ended up with an extra chair—a real pretty plastic one. And some extra Tupperware too."

Villaseñor's book, *Snow Goose Global Thanksgiving*, and its website, snowgoose.org, have inspired similar Thanksgiving events held in homes across the world, as well as in the Oceanside Amphitheater.

This year marks the 27th annual gathering founded for the purpose of "bringing all people together in a day of peace, music, dialogue, and sharing of foods from everyone's kitchen."

When I called Victor to get an update for our book, after never having contacted him before, he spontaneously invited me down to stay in his Southern California home and experience the event first-hand—proving that he still does believe we're all one family.

The only admission price is a dish prepared by warm and loving hands. I think I'll bring a pecan pie.

*Villaseñor's latest book **Our First Lady Pope** follows the author's life-altering journey after he was invited to speak to retired nuns and priests, a group whom he first needed to forgive.*

Acknowledgments

I want to thank White Cloud Press for their enthusiasm and support of our book concept. They were the first to confirm and act on, what we already believed—a book like this is needed now, and it is easy to envision a wildly successful series for years to come. Thanks to Barry Thalden who called me out of the blue, introduced me to his publisher, and offered a treasure of support.

I am grateful especially to John Conn in Montreal, who edited stories and injected vital energy and valuable time (and friendship) into our book project. Thanks also to Donna Peremes for her input and editing of content.

I am indebted to volunteers who stepped forward and committed time to tracking down people featured in stories from long ago: Carmen White, Shelby Havens, Michael Radice, and many others.

Thank you to my old friend Richard Slater, the artist and creative director who brilliantly brought our vision for this book cover to life.

I feel enormous gratitude for three brilliant writers who allowed us to reprint their stories for this collection: Dana Reinhardt, Lauri Gwilt, and the family of Brian Doyle.

Thanks to Ellen K and her competant team, Ryan and Darlene at KOST 103.5, for the FUN opportunity they give me to be on the radio every week. 'May good bless'!

I have only praise for my new partner in GNN, Anthony Samadani. He possesses so many qualities that are valuable in a co-owner: Hollywood connections, law and business acumen, zeal, faith, understanding, humor, friendliness, intelligence, strategic vision, and a great communication style that infuses goodwill in everyone he meets. I am thrilled that you (and your beautiful family) are on my team.

I thank my three kids for their understanding and forgiveness when I would arrive late for school pick-ups after being engrossed in a GNN assignment. They helped peel address stickers and put them on hundreds of newsletters. And after 9/11, when I lost faith and mentioned out loud that maybe GNN didn't even matter, 10-year-old Jack said, "No, mom. People need you now, more than ever."

And, finally (I saved the best for last), I want to thank the extraordinary McKinley Corbley. She effortlessly evolved from a personal assistant to freelance writer to managing editor, taking the reigns at a critical time in 2016 when GNN needed her most. I've often said that if she stopped working for GNN, I wouldn't be able to replace her. Thank you for your dedication, youthful perspective, genius ideas, compassionate listening, and jazzy style. You are the heartbeat of GNN—Oh, captain, my captain! xxoo